Eros es más

Eros Is More

Juan Antonio González Iglesias

Eros es más

Eros Is More

TRANSLATED BY Curtis Bauer

Alice James Books

FARMINGTON, MAINE

10 9 8 7 6 5 4 3 2 1

Alice James Books are published by Alice James Poetry Cooperative, Inc., an affiliate
of the University of Maine at Farmington.

Alice James Books
114 Prescott Street
Farmington, ME 04938
www.alicejamesbooks.org

LIBRARY OF CONGRESS CATALOGING-IN-PUBLICATION DATA
González Iglesias, Juan Antonio.
[Eros es más. English]
Eros Is More / Juan Antonio Gonázlez Iglesias ; translated by Curtis Bauer.
    pages   cm
ISBN 978-1-938584-07-7 (paperback)
I. Bauer, Curtis, 1970- translator. II. Title.
PQ6657.O5516E7613 2014
861'.64--dc 3   2014010138

Alice James Books gratefully acknowledges support from individual donors, private
foundations, the University of Maine at Farmington, and the National Endowment
for the Arts.

ART WORKS.
arts.gov

COVER ART: "Scherzo di Follia," Pierre-Louis Pierson (1822-1913), Adoc-photos /
Art Resource, NY

Contents

Acknowledgments

The translator gratefully acknowledges the following journals and magazines in which these translations first appeared (sometimes in different incarnations), and thanks their editors for their generous support of this work and of poetry in translation in general.

The American Poetry Review: "Natural Happiness," "Aikido," "Holy Thursday," "Gymnast," and "There Is Something inside Love"

Circumference: Poetry in Translation: "October, Month without Gods," "The Art of Translation," "Fulfillment"

The Common (Dispatches): "Destined for Oblivion?" and "Málaga"

The Dirty Goat: "You Light Up My Life," "Chart for the Diversity of Days," "Time Begets Decades," "American Campus," and "40"

The Hampden-Sydney Poetry Review: "Mon Tout Dans Ce Monde" and "Ars Poetica"

Indiana Review: "Stripper, Clothed"

International Poetry Review: "Young Man with Dalmatians" and "Too Many Things"

Shearsman (United Kingdom): "Question with an Answer that Doesn't Matter," "Correspondence," "In the Christian Garden," "If I Wake in the Middle of the Night," and "The Reign of Hadrian"

Thanks to Vicki Bee for her limited edition letterpress broadside of the poem "Ars Poetica."

The creation and revision of these translations were encouraged and supported by grants from Texas Tech University, The Helen Devitt Jones Foundation, and the kind patrons at Residencia Roquissar.

I would like to express my gratitude to Soledad Fox who encouraged my first attempts at this task; to my colleagues in the Creative Writing program and the Department of Classical and Modern Languages at Texas Tech University, in particular Carmen Pereira-Muro, William Wenthe, John Poch, and Adam Houle for their generous comments on this manuscript, and to Don Lavigne, Jason Banta, and David Larmour for their assistance with the Latin and references to classical texts in this collection. Thank you to Alice James Books, Meg Willing, Alyssa Neptune, Carey Salerno, and the cooperative board for believing in this book. Thank you to Steve Scafidi and Patrick Rosal for being such generous, patient, and encouraging readers, and for being such wonderful poets.

I consider myself privileged to have received such a rigorous education in Spanish language, literature, and culture from so many good people, in particular my friends and family in Spain, Mexico and Argentina. Thanks especially to Idoia Elola for her patience, and her willingness to read these translations in all their incarnations.

Finally, my deepest appreciation to Juan Antonio for trusting me with these beautiful, important poems. I am indebted to you for this gift.

Introduction to the Translation

In the summer of 2013, Juan Antonio González Iglesias invited me to Salamanca to speak with him about his poems and poetics. At that time, I had been translating his work for close to a decade and had corresponded with him frequently, but I had met him only in passing at an event where he was being inducted into the Real Academia de Bellas Artes de San Telmo in Málaga. On the train from Madrid to Salamanca I recalled a summer years before, in another part of Spain, when I first encountered his poem "Excess of Life" in the Saturday literary supplement of *El País*:

Excess of Life

I have been thinking about death since I met you.
But what I have in mind is nothing like
common sorrow. It's more like a certainty
of the totality of my days in this
world where I've been able to find you.
Suddenly I have all the impatience of everyone
who loved and loves, the unshareable urgency
of those in love. I don't want geography
but love—it is the only thing my heart knows.
In my life there is no room for this excess of life.
It would be better to tell you I meditate on things
(borders and distances) in the proper terms
of resurrection, when we will rise
over the fixed locations of time and space,
independent of the sea that separates us.
The perfect moment I dream of is the embrace,
unrushed, the kisses that have remained unkissed.
I dream that your body lives next to my body
and I wait for the morning when there will be no limits.

I immediately wanted to translate this poem for friends back in the US. This urge, as all of us who translate know, can be reason enough to take on a translation project, but what I would later discover after reading the entire collection of *Eros Is More* and then after beginning my correspondence with González Iglesias, is that there is a deeply generous voice—profoundly kind, loving, and brilliant—inside these poems; there is a speaker concerned with revealing the presence of love and honor in our daily lives that is so often hidden by the rush of modern obligations and contemporary social constraints. Ten years later, González Iglesias's invitation for me to come to his home in Salamanca showed me the true duality of his work and life: he is a tenured professor of classics at the oldest and most prestigious university in Spain (though few of his colleagues wholly understand the extent of his success in the poetry world); he has won most of the major Spanish literary prizes, written criticism for the major Spanish literary supplements and journals, and received praise throughout the Spanish literary community, yet he does not use this prestige to his advantage, rarely gives readings, and is an outsider in the country's vibrant poetry scene; he is Catholic but openly homoerotic, openly homosexual;[1] he is multilingual, doctored in classical philology and literary theory, but the language in his poems often appears simple, direct, even informal. So when I entered his home and was shown to my apartment, it made perfect sense that while the windows on one side looked onto the old city of Salamanca, the New Cathedral tower (built between the 16th and 18th centuries), and centuries-old university buildings, the view on the opposite side was of the Tormes River, the bike paths, trees and athletic fields along it, and the new city on the other side. The classical and modern, nature and man, the silence and contemplation of scholarship and faith and the noise of slow-moving water, birds in flight, leaves in the trees: examples of the "borders and distances," the things upon which he and his poems meditate and the in-between spaces he inhabits.

---

1. See notes for further discussion.

The poems in *Eros Is More* muse on the in-between. Having immersed himself in the study of Roman and Greek literature and rhetoric, many of González Iglesias's poems demonstrate a mode of contemplating classical authors through a contemporary lens, applying ancient philosophy to current situations. In his brief essay on poetics in the series *Poetics and Poetry* (Fundación Juan March, 2008), he outlines the obligation of today's poet, keeping in mind the respect Roman senators had for the intellectuals and poets of their day, as well as their obligation to use language correctly: "... poets should teach the average citizen to reject words, because behind words are things, with all their evil... Poets should set an example for the average citizen."[2] These are words to live by, and González Iglesias is a poet who expresses elemental truths in his poems. He does so by reminding us that poetry, the most perfect form of language, has deep resonance in the private life of the average citizen and in the political life of a society. "Eros," he says, "governs the physical and metaphysical reality. Eros is more than thanatos. Love is stronger than death."

How does one translate the work of a poet with such linguistic expertise and refined poetic skill as González Iglesias—a poet who requires that his readers not only consider multiple languages as they read a poem but also that they consider the contemporary world they inhabit through classical ideas? In the prologue to the Spanish edition of *Eros Is More*, he tells us that:

> . . . some words belong to the dictionary of untranslatable terms. Eros is one of them. It is one of the words that we keep saying in Greek, because some things you always say in the language of those who knew it best.

We can learn much about art and literature from the masters of its craft and, in this case, I have attempted to follow the lessons inside González Iglesias's poems. The difficulty of translating these poems

---

2. All translations of the quoted text in the introduction are my own.

does not originate from how one attempts to interpret their complex metaphors or follow the historic references; instead, it comes from how to convey the poems' tones and musicalities, and recognizing what to translate. In considering the numerous lines in Latin in a poem like "Correspondence," for example, I have to determine how and why the Latin was used in the first place: Is it the sound of the Latin when the poem is read out loud? Does the Latin act merely as an indicator of foreignness? Contextualization? Distance? My solution in this poem and others, like "Vltimus Romanorum" with its lines in Latin and English mixed with the original Spanish, has been to keep the phrases in Latin and add a Latin-to-English translation in the notes at the end of the collection. I did so because I want these English versions to exhibit the linguistic distinctions González Iglesias expresses in the Spanish.

Many poems in this collection engage seemingly contradictory ideas only to arrive at the conclusion that everything is connected, that our contemporary actions and observations run parallel to those of our past: a contemporary singer's lyrics remind the speaker of one poem of Augustine of Hippo's prayer; a lover coming in from a bike ride along the river draws another speaker back to Aristotelian philosophy. Whether through the Olympic athlete's dedication to his sport and his underlying wish to have a normal social life, or the contemplation of a bronze memorial plaque on a bench that causes the speaker in "In Joyful Memory" to consider eros and thanatos and to consider how we move through the world without fully comprehending the impact of each seemingly inconsequential movement and utterance, the poems in *Eros Is More* can be read as lessons in how to live a more observant life and speak a more deliberate language.

González Iglesias's poetic style does not fit in one particular school or tradition of Spanish poetry. His erudition and training in classics are two elements that align him with poets from the *Novísimos* tradition, a contemporary tradition characterized by the use of arresting images and narrative elements to arrive at meaning and communicate that art can awaken vitality via the positioning of their poems within prior contexts. His poetry also exhibits the influence of the *Poesía de la experiencia*. Especially indicative of this lineage, is his use of autobiographical information and his investigation of personal responses to those lived experiences. Like the *Novísimos* writers, González Iglesias's poems are acts of discovery, often meandering through a scene before arriving at a resolution or revelation at the end. They also often use levels of diction that do not correspond with our lofty ideas of classical literature—though every classical scholar can list countless examples of the sordidness of Catullus and Martial—as well as incorporate different languages and myths to provide an authoritative and historic framework. The poem "In Joyful Memory," as a case in point, begins with a simple reflection on a memorial for someone the speaker doesn't know; however, it quickly moves outward with the grandiose statement "*Love is stronger than death,*" which not only alludes to the central dialectic in this collection—the relationship between eros and thanatos—but also touches on a central component of González Iglesias's poetics: that we can encounter a mix of both high and low diction in a "noble" poem...because language is what we all possess, what we all have the ability to transform, what all of us can adapt to our lives and use to be memorable. At the same time, there is a definite speaker who relates the experiences and emotions; here the speaker realizes:

> That's how we write, without really knowing
> what we want to say, what these
> rare words mean, repeated
> by the generations of men.

Through the contemplation inside this poem, the speaker arrives at a series of epiphanies or conclusions about himself; the poet, however, does not articulate this arrival explicitly, but instead concludes by broadening the poem's scope so that we may move beyond the personal to consider how society might also arrive at some deeper understanding. The event of a stranger's death helps the speaker construct a link to a larger metaphysical issue:

> [. . .] It's like this. Love is more.
> And it will triumph in a mysterious way.
> That's why we have it engraved in bronze:
> love is stronger than death.

This simple statement, that love is stronger than death, is central to all the poems in *Eros Is More*. Although these poems illustrate multiple levels of distance and separation, allowing us to discern that our interactions parallel interactions throughout the history of human relationships, they also reveal that love is central to the function of the world. For González Iglesias, love affects every human being, no matter what social or cultural status, no matter what age. The Greek concept of eros refers to the strength of union between all beings. These poems are just as attentive to the contemporary athlete, stripper, or dead stranger as they are to the ancient Romans and Greeks; this poet wants us to realize that every subject is equally poetic and as deserving of attention as the elevated word "eros" in the title. A poet who has an interest in—and inhabits—both classical and contemporary themes, is a poet who deserves study, a poet we will learn from. I am fortunate that Juan Antonio has trusted me to convey his poems to an English-speaking readership.

Curtis Bauer
LUBBOCK, TEXAS

Eros es más

Eros Is More

Exceso de Vida

Desde que te conozco tengo en cuenta la muerte.
Pero lo que presiento no se parece en nada
a la común tristeza. Más bien es certidumbre
de la totalidad de mis días en este
mundo donde he podido encontrarme contigo.
De pronto tengo toda la impaciencia de todos
los que amaron y aman, la urgencia incompartible
de los enamorados. No quiero geografía
sino amor, es lo único que mi corazón sabe.
En mi vida no cabe este exceso de vida.
Mejor, si te dijera que medito las cosas
(fronteras y distancias) en los términos propios
de la resurrección, cuando nos alzaremos
sobre las coordenadas del tiempo y el espacio,
independientemente del mar que nos separa.
Sueño con el momento perfecto del abrazo
sin prisa, de los besos que quedaron sin darse.
Sueño con que tu cuerpo vive junto a mi cuerpo
y espero la mañana en la que no habrá límites.

Excess of Life

I have been thinking about death since I met you.
But what I have in mind is nothing like
common sorrow. It's more like a certainty
of the totality of my days in this
world where I've been able to find you.
Suddenly I have all the impatience of everyone
who loved and loves, the unshareable urgency
of those in love. I don't want geography
but love—it is the only thing my heart knows.
In my life there is no room for this excess of life.
It would be better to tell you I meditate on things
(borders and distances) in the proper terms
of resurrection, when we will rise
over the fixed locations of time and space,
independent of the sea that separates us.
The perfect moment I dream of is the embrace,
unrushed, the kisses that have remained unkissed.
I dream that your body lives next to my body
and I wait for the morning when there will be no limits.

Mon Tout Dans Ce Monde

Palabras de otro idioma, de otro siglo,
de otro amor: aceptarlas
para poder decir cómo te quiero,
lo que eres para mí.
Exactamente eso: mi todo en este mundo.

Mon Tout Dans Ce Monde

Words from another language, from another century,
from another love: to accept them
in order to say how I love you,
what you mean to me.
Exactly this: my everything in this world.

Misántropo, Ma Non Troppo

Que no te pase a ti con los misántropos
lo mismo que a los hombres con los hombres.
Marco Aurelio, *Meditaciones, 7*

Durante veinte años he tratado
con muy pocas personas. Desatento
a todo lo que no fuera solsticio
o equinoccio,
en la soberanía del invierno
y el verano
celebraba mis fiestas
esperándote.
Adonde me invitaban no acudí.
¿El motivo? Uno solo:
me concentro mejor en un ciprés
que en las conversaciones.
Así he concluido
que cada árbol es un incontable
como el agua.
Así son cada vez más las personas
a las que quiero mucho y veo poco.
Un ángulo me basta,
un libro y un amigo, un sueño breve.
Tiempo para el amor es lo que pido.
En los actos sociales pienso en ti.
Casi siempre
entre el ruido de copas, de palabras,
llega cierto momento en el que pienso:
Necesito urgentemente ver a un limpio de corazón.
Hablar con él. Guardarme entre sus brazos.

Misanthrope, Ma Non Troppo

*Take care that you don't feel for the misanthropes
the same way that humans too often feel toward each other.*
Marcus Aurelius, *Meditations*, 7

For twenty years I have interacted
with very few people. Inattentive
to everything that was not solstice
or equinox,
in the sovereignty of winter
and summer
I celebrated my festivals
waiting for you.
I didn't go where I was invited.
The reason? Just one:
I concentrate better on a cypress
than on conversations.
In this way I've come to the conclusion
that each tree is uncountable
like water.
In this way there are always more people
I love deeply but see less and less.
One angle is enough for me,
one book and one friend, a quick nap.
Time for love is what I ask for.
I think of you during social events.
Almost always
between the clinking of glasses, of words,
a certain moment arrives that I think:
I urgently need to see a pure heart.
Talk with him. Settle into his arms.

Descansar mi cabeza
encima de la roja frecuencia de su vida.
Únicamente esto:
que en los actos sociales pienso en ti.

Rest my head
on the red frequency of his life.
Only this:
that I think of you during social events.

Contracandela

. . . en las plantaciones de caña de azúcar, fuego
que se da, en caso de incendio, en la parte del
cañaveral de donde viene el viento, para que, al
llegar allí las llamas, queden detenidas.
    Diccionario ideológico de la lengua española de Julio Casares

Leer el diccionario como un libro de horas.
Buscar en los residuos del idioma algún símbolo
que pudiera servirme para acreditar
claridad. Repetir como una letanía:
te conozco, eres Eros, el mismo que de antiguo
arrasa por la vida y la literatura.
No ceder a las lógicas expresiones de pánico.
Fiarme una vez más de las viejas metáforas,
Comprendiendo que ésta de los cañaverales
—plantaciones y viento y llamas detenidas—
sirve bien a los días vulnerables de un hombre.

Fire Break

> *... on the sugarcane plantations, fire that's lit,*
> *in case of a fire, on the side of the cane bed*
> *from where the wind comes, so that, once*
> *the flames arrive, they will be stopped.*
> from Julio Casares's *Diccionario ideológico de la lengua española*

Read the dictionary like a book of hours.
Look for some symbol in the residue of language
that might help me confirm
clarity. Repeat like a litany:
I know you, you are Eros, the same one that has for so long
devastated life and literature.
Do not give in to the logical expressions of panic.
Trust once more in the old metaphors,
understanding that this one about the cane beds
—plantations and wind and flames held back—
serves the vulnerable days of one man well.

Teoría de la Fiesta

La fiesta se parece al universo
en que es única.
No es tripartita como la Comedia
de Dante. No resulta
posible discernir un paraíso
en su interior, y menos distinguir
entre los bienaventurados y los malos.
Platón dice que el cosmos es un gran animal.
Extraterritorial, así es la fiesta.
Guarda una relación inexplicable con el poder
por eso algunos piensan en la belleza de las formas de gobierno
mientras se incorporan a la elasticidad de ser muchos.
Los cuerpos recuperan una soberanía
anterior a los nombres del registro
y algunos improvisan nomenclaturas nuevas
para individuarlos,
una vez que se ha revelado inservible la serie de los números naturales,
o la reiteración del santoral sobre las cabezas perfectas.
Qué difícil se hace precisar lo que tiene
de profecía
la fiesta.
Bullicio de la especie en torno a ningún centro.
Uno de mis alumnos la define
insuperablemente
                    como exhibición
de volúmenes.

Fiesta Theory

The fiesta is like the universe—
there is nothing else like it.
It isn't tripartite like Dante's
Comedy. It isn't possible
to distinguish a paradise
in its interior, and less so to distinguish
between the chosen and the damned.
Plato says the cosmos is a great animal.
Extraterritorial, that's what the fiesta is like.
It keeps an unfathomable relationship with power,
that's why some think of beauty in forms of government
while they join in the elasticity of numbers.
Bodies recuperate a sovereignty
before the names on the register
and some improvise new taxonomies
to individualize them
once the series of natural numbers has been revealed as useless,
or the reiteration of the calendar of saints' days above the perfect heads.
How difficult it is to need to specify what
prophecy there is
in the fiesta.
Hubbub of the kind around no center.
One of my students defines it
unsurpassably
                as an exhibition
of volumes.

You Light Up My Life

Aristóteles dice: un cuerpo bello
debe de ser percibido en su totalidad.
Así te vi llegar esta mañana.
Venías de correr una hora en bici
por la orilla del río. Te duchaste.
Estuvimos nadando juntos. Varios
largos en la piscina transparente.
Nos amamos después, enamorados
de ser distintos y de ser iguales.
Por la tarde estudiabas o escribías.
Te vi algunos instantes. Pero ahora
que duermes a mi lado respirando
desnudo en el calor de junio, a oscuras,
creo que el filósofo no se refiere
sólo a la epifanía en el espacio,
al golpe único de la materia,
sino también al cuerpo hecho de tiempo,
a la suma sencilla de momentos
que queda para siempre en el registro
general de los días de este mundo.
Aristóteles dice: un cuerpo bello
debe ser percibido en su totalidad.

You Light Up My Life

Aristotle says: a beautiful body
should be observed in its totality.
That's how I saw you arrive this morning.
You came in from riding your bike, an hour
along the river bank. You showered.
We swam together. Several
lengths in the pool's transparence.
We made love afterwards, in love
with being different and being the same.
In the afternoon you studied or wrote.
I saw you for a few moments. But now
that you sleep beside me breathing
naked in the June heat, in the dark,
I think the philosopher doesn't only
refer to the epiphany in space,
to the lone blow of matter,
but also to the body made of time,
to the simple sum of moments
that will stay forever in the general
register of this world's days.
Aristotle says: a beautiful body
should be observed in its totality.

Tabla de la Diversidad de los Días

(nombre de una tabla de navegación regalada
por Nebrija a Hernando Colón)

Bien mirado, el otoño pertenece
a la categoría
de los placeres infrecuentes, esos
cuyo filo no debe desgastarse
por el uso. Y no existe
belleza independiente del esplendor distinto
de las cuatro estaciones.
Si ahora me pusiera
a dibujar un cuadrifolio,
nos mostraría como un excesivo
enamorado de lo concreto.
¿Quién describe el efecto detallado
que tiene el mundo sobre nuestros días?
Una equivalencia abstracta
resulta más satisfactoria.
También más eficaz.
Ojalá el año solamente fuera
una rotación completa
del pensamiento, eso
—lo mismo exactamente—que
según Paul Valéry
es un poema.

Chart for the Diversity of Days

*(the name of a navigation chart given
to Ferdinand Columbus by Nebrija)*

Closely observed, autumn belongs
to the category
of those infrequent pleasures, those
whose blades won't dull
from use. And beauty
doesn't exist independent of the distinct splendor
of the four seasons.
If right now I tried
to draw a quadrifolium,
it would show us madly
in love with the concrete.
Who describes the detailed effect
the world has on our days?
An abstract correspondence
seems more fitting.
And more effective.
I wish the year were only
a complete rotation
of thought, that—
the exact same thing—which
according to Paul Valéry
is called a poem.

Octubre, Mes sin Dioses

Los japoneses piensan que éste es el mes-sin-dioses.
Lo celebran así. No aliteran octubre
con oro desprendido de los árboles frágiles,
ni con revoluciones que cambiaron la historia.
Octubre como tregua. Como ausencia de todo
lo que excede los límites. Así para nosotros
sea: liberación. Porque ya no se exhiben
los implacables dioses desnudos del verano,
los demasiados dioses, y falta todavía
mucho para que nazca el niño del invierno,
y más allá no alcanza la vista, desde este
mes de distancias, mes de lejanías,
imperfecto, logrado, fortuito. Que así
sea para nosotros. Sin los ocho millones
de dioses que se esconden en la ciudad o el bosque,
las escalas coinciden con nuestras estaturas.
Dejémonos llevar por los presentimientos.
Escribamos las cosas con las letras minúsculas.
Celebremos octubre por su ausencia de dioses.
Disfrutemos su nombre porque sólo es un número
de una serie truncada. Y olvidada. Es octubre.
Tenemos treinta días sólo para nosotros.

October, Month without Gods

The Japanese think this is the month-without-gods.
They celebrate it this way. They don't alliterate October
with gold falling from the fragile trees,
or with revolutions that changed history.
October, like a truce. Like an absence of everything
that exceeds limits. May it be for us
liberation. Because now they don't exhibit
the relentless naked gods of summer,
the too many gods, and so much remains
for the child of winter to be born,
and our sight doesn't reach any further, from this
month of distances, month of far aways,
imperfect, attained, fortuitous. If only it would be
like this for us. Without the eight million
gods that hide in the city or in the forest,
the scales coincide with our statures.
Let us be carried away by our premonitions.
Let us write things with small letters.
Let us celebrate October for its absence of gods.
Let us enjoy its name because it is only a number
in a truncated series. And forgotten. It is October.
We have thirty days all to ourselves.

Doncel con Dálmata

Con la seguridad de los que han sido
dibujados por una sola línea,
delante de la pétrea
catedral se desplazan
elásticos. Por ser
mutuo regalo desde el primer día,
van sin saberlo dando
sentido a los jardines. Sus insonorizadas
zancadas de *nike air* extralimitan
a los contemplativos. A lo lejos
se pierden por la orilla
del río como una
única
criatura.

Young Man with Dalmatian

With the certainty of those who have been
drawn by a single line,
in front of the stone
cathedral they move around
with elasticity. Just being
a mutual gift from the first day,
they go about without knowing it, giving
meaning to the gardens. The soundless
strides of his *Nike Airs* overstep
the contemplative. In the distance
they get lost on the river
bank like a
unique
creature.

Arte Poética

Si no quieres quedarte a mirar la tormenta,
yo la miro por ti.

Ars Poetica

If you don't want to stay and watch the storm,
I will watch it for you.

Cuestión cuya Respuesta No Importa

para Christian Law Palacín

Se pregunta el teólogo
medieval si dos ángeles
pueden
hablar—comunicarse—
sin que los otros ángeles los oigan.
No importa la respuesta
sino la sensación
casi física
de que bajo esos códigos simbólicos
se dibuja una exacta
definición de cómo
funciona la poesía
transmitida en especie
de libro, y este raro
placer que proporcionan
las cosas del espíritu
siempre
que se escriba en minúscula.

Question with an Answer that Doesn't Matter

for Christian Law Palacín

A medieval theologian asks
if two angels
can
speak—converse—
without the other angels hearing them.
The answer doesn't matter
but the almost
physical sensation
that beneath these symbolic codes
one can draw an exact
definition of how
poetry can be
transmitted
in book form, and this strange
pleasure
that spiritual things allow
provided
that they are written in lower case.

Ha Estado en la Vendimia

para mi madre

Ha estado en la vendimia. Dice que se parece
a un ejercicio zen.

"Primero todos gritan, están como excitados.
Como si presintieran una embriaguez futura
mientras se distribuyen por la tierra. Tú mismo
oyes y dices cosas que nunca imaginaste.
Te pierdes en tu surco, cada uno en el suyo,
manejas la hoz pequeña, vacías los capazos
en el remolque. Vuelves a tu lugar y entras
en un silencio enorme. Las horas, los minutos
dejan de numerarse, sería tan inútil
como contar las uvas, pero al final del día
sabes exactamente qué partes de tu cuerpo
van a dolerte."

Ha estado en la vendimia.
Dice que se parece a un ejercicio zen.

She Has Been at the Grape Harvest

for my mother

She has been at the grape harvest. She says it's like
a Zen exercise.

"First, everyone shouts as if they were excited.
As if they had a premonition of future inebriation
as they spread out over the land. Even you
hear and say things you would have never imagined.
You lose yourself in your row, everyone in his own,
you maneuver the small sickle, empty the baskets
in the wagon. You go back to your place and enter
that enormous silence. The hours, the minutes
stop numbering off, it would be as useless
as counting the grapes, but at the end of the day
you know exactly which parts of your body
will hurt."

      She has been at the grape harvest.
She says it's like a Zen exercise.

Felicidad Natural

para Ángeles Pérez López

Es bueno para el cuerpo contemplar los trigales
verdes esta mañana de principio de mayo.
Es bueno para el cuerpo imaginar
que esta alta pradera, tan sometida al viento
que parece estar hecha sólo del mismo viento,
no terminara nunca en una suma
de áridas aristas.
Es bueno para el cuerpo que el único sonido
sea
el rumor de la lluvia sobre el techo del coche.
Es bueno para el cuerpo detenerse.
Y salir.
En un punto indeterminado de esta península, la más
　　　　occidental de Europa,
recuerdo la liturgia de la Iglesia de Oriente,
que en el momento de la comunión
se limita a decir:
lo bueno,
para los buenos.

Natural Happiness

for Ángeles Pérez López

It is good for the body to see the wheat fields
green this morning at the beginning of May.
It is good for the body to imagine
that this high meadow, so completely given to the wind
that it seems to be made only of wind,
would never end in any sum
of arid edges.
It is good for the body that the only sound
be
the rumor of rain on the car roof.
It is good for the body to stop.
And get out.
In an undefined place on this peninsula, the furthest
        west in Europe,
I remember the liturgy of the Eastern Orthodox Church
that in the moment of communion
the only thing said is:
that which is good,
for those who are good.

Demasiadas Cosas

para Christian

El asceta es consciente de demasiadas cosas.
Un exceso de amor lo amarra al mundo.
Cada casualidad se convierte en un vínculo.
Siente cada palabra, cada letra.
Se puede enamorar de una definición
encontrada al azar en cualquier diccionario.
A veces tiene miedo de que su corazón alcance el tamaño
     del cosmos.
Por eso con paciencia va deshaciendo nudos.
Corta ataduras. Se le va la vida
en desentenderse.

Too Many Things

for Christian

The ascetic is conscious of too many things.
An excess of love moors him to the world.
Each coincidence turns into a link.
He feels each word, each letter.
He can fall in love with a definition
found by chance in any dictionary.
Sometimes he's afraid his heart will grow to the size
        of the cosmos.
That's why he undoes the knots so patiently.
He cuts tethers. His life is spent
disentangling himself.

El Tiempo Engendra Décadas

en memoria de Rafael Pérez Estrada

El Tiempo engendra décadas
lo mismo que el Poder engendra caballos.
Que nadie se lamente
de su velocidad.
Aunque aquella admirable
unidad de medida
que Tito Livio usó para narrar la Historia de Roma desde
        su fundación,
parece algo desproporcionada
para distribuir
la vida de cualquiera de nosotros.

Time Begets Decades

in memory of Rafael Pérez Estrada

Time begets decades
the same way Power generates horses.
No one should lament
its velocity.
Even though that admirable
unit of measurement
that Titus Livy used to narrate the *History of Rome*
            from its origins
seems somewhat disproportionate
to arrange
the life of any one of us.

Campus Americano

University of Oregon

Entre la biblioteca y el gimnasio
se extiende el cementerio donde duermen
los que fundaron la ciudad. El musgo
crece por las mayúsculas romanas
de los nombres británicos, y dentro
de los exactos números el liquen
obstruye la lectura: *Died September.*
Consigo descifrar que alguien vivió
28 años 17 días
en el siglo pasado, el XIX.
Apenas una cruz, algún ciprés.
Hiedra por todas partes. Instantáneas
corren irreverentes las ardillas
sobre las tumbas. Y por los caminos
algunas bicicletas, estudiantes
con los monopatines y los libros
bajo el brazo, y el tránsito esperable
de enamorados y de solitarios.
Yo mismo lo atravieso muchas veces.
Los jueves por la tarde los alumnos
juegan en la pradera colindante
un partido de rugby que terminan
felices y agotados. Todo indica,
por el conocimiento que tenemos
de este mundo, que un día sus magníficos
muslos descansarán bajo la tierra.
Pero la sobredosis de futuro
propia de cualquier campus y la idea

American Campus

University of Oregon

Between the gymnasium and the library
the cemetery lengthens—those who founded
the city sleep there. The moss
creeps over the capital Roman letters
of the British names, and the lichen inside
the precise numbers obstructs
my reading: *Died September.*
I can decipher that someone lived
28 years, 17 days
in the last century, the XIX.
Hardly a cross, a few cypress trees.
Ivy everywhere. Instantly
the irreverent squirrels run
over the graves. And a few bicycles
on the paths, students
with skateboards and books
under their arms, and the expected
movement of lovers and loners.
I too have crossed this place many times.
Thursday afternoons the students
play a rugby match
on the adjoining field—they finish
happy and exhausted. Everything shows,
through this knowledge that we have
of this world, that one day their magnificent
thighs will rest under the earth.
But an overdose of the future
on any campus and the idea

de que las leyes físicas no tienen
plena vigencia en este territorio,
me hacen pensar en la resurrección
con una intensidad inusitada.
Tal vez también influya que este otoño
acabo de cumplir cuarenta años.

that the laws of physics don't have
full validity in this area,
makes me think of the resurrection
with unusual intensity.
It could also be that this fall
I have just turned forty.

Los Ojos del Asceta

Cuando algo consigue todavía
cuando alguien consigue
que vuelva la cabeza,
celebro fugazmente
cada contemplación,
porque sé que a partir
del año cuadragésimo de vida
los ojos del asceta
apenas miran ya las cosas de este mundo.

The Eyes of the Ascetic

When something can still make me,
when someone can make me
turn my head
I celebrate briefly
each glance,
because I know that after
the fortieth year of life
the eyes of the ascetic
now hardly look at the things of this world.

Stripper Vestido

Al vestirse ha hecho voto de pobreza.
Acaba de entrar en el tiempo lineal de la historia.
Ha intentado apagar
la irradiación que emite
el cuerpo pleno. Procura
administrar lo sobrenatural
que preserva o presagia
la suma de sus músculos.
Ignora de algún modo
que en hebreo, en la Biblia,
la idea misma de gloria
está asociada al peso.
De algún modo lo sabe.
Deambula melancólico
por el local oscuro.
Su misterio no puede reducirse
a la ausencia de danza.
Para abrazarse a otro
se ha revestido de deliberada
vulgaridad. En vano.
No se le acerca nadie.

Stripper, Clothed

He takes a vow of poverty when he puts on his clothes.
He's just entered the linear time line of history.
He has tried to put out
the radiance his whole body
emits. He tries
to administrate the supernatural
that preserves or announces
the sum of his muscles.
He somehow ignores
that in Hebrew, in the Bible,
the true idea of glory
is connected to weight.
Somehow he knows this.
He takes a melancholy stroll
through the dive bar.
His mystery can't be reduced
to the absence of dance.
In order to embrace another
he has put his clothes back on—
such deliberate vulgarity. In vain.
No one comes to him.

Es la Segunda Vez

Es la segunda vez que me lo encuentro
y en el mismo lugar. Junto a la *School
of Music.* En el pico
sujeta una bellota, alguna baya
que se resiste.
Su breve cuerpo es más
azul que las cabinas telefónicas
de *Qwest.* Más esplendente
que aquel coche color
azul metalizado.
Y más que la señal del carril bici.
Cuando levanta el vuelo
su fugaz trayectoria
es más azul que el cielo de este día
luminoso de octubre.

It Is the Second Time

It is the second time that I find it
and in the same place. Beside the School
of Music. It holds an acorn
in its beak, some berry
it can't open.
Its brief body is bluer
than the Qwest
telephone booths. More radiant
than that metallic
blue car.
More than the sign for the bike lane.
When it takes flight
its rapid trajectory
is bluer than the sky this
luminous October day.

Difícilmente

Entre los datos de la erudición
brota cierta tristeza
difícilmente compartible ¿a quién
puedo explicarle todo
lo que implica este artículo
de André Chastel,
publicado en inglés, el mismo año
en el que terminaba la II
Guerra Mundial,
monográficamente dedicado
a la melancolía en los sonetos
de Lorenzo el Magnífico?

Difficultly

Among the particulars of erudition
buds a certain sadness
difficultly shared. To whom
can I explain everything
in this article
by André Chastel,
published in English, the same year
as the end of the Second
World War,
dedicated in monograph
to the Melancholy in the Sonnets
of Lorenzo the Magnificent?

Vltimus Romanorum

para Rafael León

En el último disco Robbie Williams
canta aquellas palabras memorables
que con apenas diecinueve años
pronunció en África Agustín de Hipona.
Tal vez las musitó casi en silencio,
Mientras la Antigüedad se terminaba.
La más humana de las oraciones,
la que probablemente ha conmovido
como ninguna a su destinatario.
Ahora que también algo se termina,
Robbie Williams dirige su micrófono
hacia la multitud, que sin saberlo
repite la plegaria de aquel joven
romano apasionado y la propaga
en videoclips y en radios y en iPods.
La más humana de las oraciones:
Da mihi castitatem, continentiam,
sed noli modo. Oh Lord,
make me pure—but not yet.
Dame la castidad, la continencia.
Hazme puro, Señor,
pero no todavía.

Vltimus Romanorum

for Rafael León

On his latest CD Robbie Williams
sings those memorable words
that Augustine of Hippo pronounced
in Africa when he was barely nineteen.
Maybe he muttered them almost inaudibly,
while Antiquity came to an end.
The most humane of his prayers,
the one which probably moved
its audience like no other.
Now that something else also ends,
Robbie Williams directs his microphone
toward the crowd that, without knowing it,
repeats the prayer of that impassioned
young Roman, and it spreads
through video and radios and iPods.
The most humane of his discourses:
Da mihi castitatem, continentiam,
sed noli modo. Hazme puro,
Señor, pero no todavía.
Give me chastity and continence.
Make me pure, oh Lord,
but not yet.

Málaga

para María Victoria Atencia

Todas y cada una de las cosas
del mundo tienen hoy exactitud
matinal. Esta dulce luz de Málaga
declara una vez más la equivalencia
entre la realidad y el paraíso.
Está el pequeño hotel en la subida
al monte donde se alza el santuario
que toma el nombre de una diosa antigua
para honrar a María. En el jardín
hay dos pequeñas mesas preparadas
con los dones más simples. Agua. Leche.
El vidrio, diferente del cristal.
Superior al cristal. La brisa en torno.
La jarra con el zumo de naranja.
El limón al alcance de la mano,
en el árbol. Los frutos más nutricios.
El cruasán recién hecho y el pan tierno.
Sal, aceite de oliva, mermelada.
La cortesía de los anfitriones.
Una sentencia antigua que comprendo
íntegramente ahora: si no hay
amenidad, la vida no es humana.
El valle entre los montes. La ciudad
que desde aquí parece silenciosa.
Promesa es la jornada que se inicia
bajo esta cobertura de palmeras.

Málaga

for María Victoria Atencia

All and everything
in this world has clarity
today. This sweet Málaga light
declares, once again, the equivalence
between reality and paradise.
The little hotel on the climb up
to the mountain where the sanctuary stands
with the name of an old goddess
to honor Mary. In the garden
there are two little tables prepared
in the simplest manner. Water. Milk.
The glass, not quite like crystal.
Better than crystal. The breeze surrounding.
The pitcher of orange juice.
Lemons within arm's reach
on the tree. The most nutritious fruit.
Fresh croissants and warm bread.
Salt, olive oil, marmalade.
The politeness of the hosts.
An old maxim that I understand
completely now: if there is no
pleasantry, life is not human.
The valley between the mountains. The city
that seems silent from here.
Promise is the day that begins
beneath this cover of palm trees.

¿Destinados al Olvido?

Álvaro Mutis habla lentamente.
Una entrevista en un canal hispano.
Me interesa el desgaste de las cosas.
Me interesa el desgaste de los héroes.
El tono coloquial hace posible
estas palabras: *Somos destinados*
al olvido. A olvidar
y a que nos olviden.
Y así está bien.
Necesito salir. Llueve en el campus.
Llego al sencillo banco de madera
donado por aquellos que te amaron.
Otra vez leo la inscripción pequeña
como tarjeta de visita en bronce:
In loving memory
En memoria de Justin A. Colonna
Son, brother & friend
Feb, 16, 1976—Dec, 8, 1999.
Leo tu claro nombre de italiano
patricio en este extremo de occidente,
mientras octubre se concreta en húmedas
hojas caídas sobre el banco donde
se habrán sentado tantos estudiantes.
Me viene al corazón el verso homérico
que compara a los hombres con las hojas.
También, nos aseguran los biólogos,
constituye el otoño una segunda
primavera. Es probable que se cumplan
las palabras de un padre de la Iglesia
que afirmó *"Todo en la naturaleza*

Destined for Oblivion?

Álvaro Mutis speaks slowly.
It's an interview on a Hispanic channel.
I'm interested in the depletion of things.
I'm interested in the depletion of heroes.
The colloquial tone makes these words
possible: *We are destined*
for oblivion. To forget
and to be forgotten.
And that's alright.
I need to go out. It's raining on campus.
I come to the simple wood bench
donated by those who loved you.
I read the little inscription again,
like a bronze visiting card:
In loving memory
En memoria de Justin A. Colonna
Son, brother, & friend
Feb. 16, 1976—Dec. 8, 1999.
I read your clearly patrician Italian surname
on this extremity of the west,
while October becomes more tangible
in wet fallen leaves on the bench where
so many students have rested.
A Homeric verse wells up in my heart
that compares men to leaves.
And the biologists assure us that
Autumn means a second
Spring. This is most likely the fulfillment of
the words of some Church father
who affirmed, *"Everything in nature*

nos anticipa la resurrección."
Por si acaso, escribimos, por si es cierto.
Por si el olvido fuera un episodio
provisional en nuestro largo viaje.
En medio de esta lluvia quién sabría
si somos destinados al olvido.
Tengo en cuenta el amor, el bronce, el breve
número de tus años y comprendo
que a mí, que no sé nada de tus días,
me corresponde ahora recordarte.

anticipates the resurrection."
Just in case it's true, we write.
In case oblivion were a provisional
episode on our long journey.
In the middle of this rain who would know
if we are destined for oblivion.
I have love in mind, bronze, the brief
number of your years, and I understand
that it's up to me, who knows nothing
about your days, to remember you right now.

Correspondencia

En esta biblioteca americana
acompaña mi tarde
una edición de las *Meditaciones*
de Marco Aurelio, *Marcus
Antoninus imperator
ad se ipsum,* seguida
de su correspondencia
con Frontón. Varias cartas
cruzadas entre el príncipe
y el profesor, que siempre
se dirige a su alumno
respetuosamente:
Domino Antonino Augusto.
En sus respuestas, el Emperador
es aún más sencillo.
Sólo escribe:
Magistro.

Correspondence

I'm joined this afternoon
in this American library
by an edition of the *Meditations*
of Marcus Aurelius—*Marcus
Antoninus imperator
ad se ipsum*, according to
his correspondence
with Fronto. Numerous letters
were exchanged between the prince
and teacher, who always
addressed his student
respectfully:
Domino Antonino Augusto.
In his replies, the Emperor
is even more direct.
He writes, simply:
Magistro.

En el Jardín Cristiano

Había un jardín árabe. Otro jardín cristiano.
Parecía un palacio soñado sobriamente
para otros aristócratas. Era una fundación
en el centro remoto de una isla en el centro
del mar. Los propietarios eran dos arquitectos.
Conocían los nombres de cada planta rara
en idiomas distintos, y en el latín botánico.
Recorrimos con calma una ligeramente
extravagante y magna colección de pintura.
Y admiramos el lujo secreto de su casa.
Cuando ya nos marchábamos hacia nuestra rutina,
alguien me tendió un fruto en el jardín cristiano,
recién mordido, gotas de la fruta y su boca.
Me gustó lo que nunca antes me había gustado.

In the Christian Garden

There was an Arab garden. And another Christian one.
It seemed like a palace dreamed of soberly
for other aristocrats. It was a foundation
in the remote center of an island in the middle
of the ocean. The owners were two architects.
They knew the names of every rare plant
in different languages, and in botanical Latin.
We walked calmly around a slightly
extravagant and large collection of paintings.
And we admired the secret luxury of their house.
Then, when we were getting ready to return to our routines,
someone handed me a piece of recently bitten fruit
in the Christian garden, drops from the fruit and his mouth.
I liked what I had never liked before.

Si Me Despierto en Medio de la Noche

Si me despierto en medio de la noche,
me basta con tocarte.
A mi lado respira
tu cuerpo de hombre joven
como animal en la naturaleza.
A mi lado descansa
esta musculatura construida
en la constancia del entrenamiento.
El tenista que triunfa
en las pistas de barrio cada martes,
el artista, el poeta, el que redacta
su tesis doctoral, el que diseña
el que canta, el que baila,
el que sonríe deslumbrantemente
el que guarda silencio,
el que lee,
el que combate contra mí en la cama,
el compañero de todas mis horas
tiene en estos momentos la perfección distinta.
La alegría, la gracia
que en las horas solares constituye
belleza que se mueve
ahora se resuelve en equilibrio.
Me gusta estar a ciegas.
No existe nada más que tu temperatura
resumiendo los datos verdaderos del mundo.
En medio de la noche,
tengo de pronto un indeterminado
número de minutos
para quererte

If I Wake in the Middle of the Night

If I wake in the middle of the night,
touching you is enough.
Your young man's body
breathes at my side
like a free animal.
This musculature constructed
out of constant training
rests by my side.
The tennis player who triumphs
on the public courts every Tuesday,
the artist, the poet, the one who writes
his dissertation, the one who designs,
the one who sings, the one who dances,
the one who smiles dazzlingly,
the one who remains silent,
the one who reads,
the one who struggles with me in bed,
the companion of all my hours
has in these moments a different perfection.
The happiness, the grace
that in the sun-filled hours composes
the beauty that moves
is now solved in equilibrium.
I like to be in the dark.
Nothing exists but your temperature
summarizing the true facts of the world.
In the middle of the night,
I suddenly have an indeterminate
number of minutes
to love you

con el aturdimiento y la clarividencia
de los desvelados.
Siento en tu piel al ser humano bueno.
El ritmo de tu aliento
me comunica música muy simple.
Me indica mi lugar
en el cosmos. Al lado
de tu serenidad viril. Empiezo
a quedarme dormido
abrazado a tu cuerpo.
Si me despierto en medio de la noche,
me basta con tocarte.

with the bewilderment and lucidity
of someone wide awake.
I feel the good being in your skin.
The rhythm of your breath
sings to me the simplest music.
It indicates my place
in the cosmos. Beside
your virile serenity. I begin
to fall asleep
embracing your body.
If I wake in the middle of the night,
touching you is enough.

Aikido

para Carmen Codoñer

Estamos preparados
para sobreponernos.
Es un arte. Se aprende.
Está en nuestra memoria desde niños.
Los juegos, los poemas,
las tardes traduciendo,
palabra por palabra,
las tragedias, el cruento
latín de historiadores.
Todo va al corazón y, transcurridas
las décadas, se vuelve
serenidad. Y ahora
alguno de los textos
de los filósofos occidentales
que he leído estos días
me lleva hasta la fórmula
que con la reverencia
mutua se intercambian
discípulo y maestro en el aikido.
Uno a otro se dicen:
Gracias por enseñarme

Aikido

for Carmen Codoñer

We are ready
to overcome.
It's an art. Learned.
It's in our memory from childhood.
The games, the poems,
the afternoons translating,
word for word,
the tragedies, the bloody
Latin of historians.
Everything taken to heart and, as the decades
go by, they become
serene. And now
one of the texts
of the Western philosophers
that I have been reading these days
leads me to the formula
of mutual reverence
the disciple and master
exchange in the aikido.
One says to the other:
Thank you for teaching me.

40

A los cuarenta años Djuna Barnes,
harta de todo tipo
de excesos, se encerró
en su pequeño apartamento y nunca
más se movió de allí durante otras
cuatro décadas.
A los cuarenta años Marco Polo
volvió de su aventura por Oriente.
Le quedaba anotar
pacientemente tantos exotismos:
todas las maravillas en un libro.
A los cuarenta años Elio Adriano
después de sus estudios
de latín y de griego
y de haber recorrido
etapa por etapa
la formación completa de un romano,
consideró que estaba preparado
ya para gobernar.

40

At forty Djuna Barnes,
tired of all types
of excess, closed herself up
in her little apartment and never
left there again for
another four decades.
At forty Marco Polo
returned from his adventure in the Orient.
He still had to set down,
patiently, all the exotic facts:
all the marvels in a book.
At forty Elio Adriano
after his study
of Latin and Greek
and after pouring over,
phase by phase,
the complete formation of a Roman,
considered himself, then
prepared to govern.

Cumplimiento

El oráculo dijo
que para ser feliz
debería vivir en una casa
levantada sobre un lugar que no
estuviera ni dentro
ni fuera
de la ciudad.

Yo he cumplido mi parte.

Fulfillment

The oracle said
that in order to be happy
you should live in a house
raised above a place that is
neither inside nor
outside
the city.

I've done my part.

El Reinado de Adriano

Se trata, sobre todo, de una teoría del conocimiento,
del modo en que un hombre se sustrae poco a poco a
las ideas de su tiempo, que rechaza.
       Marguerite Yourcenar, [sobre Zenón], *Carta a Alain Bosquet,*
       1 de enero de 1964

El reinado de Adriano
se parece al octubre que celebran
los japoneses. Pero la nostalgia
que siento de esos años no se debe
a la ausencia de dioses. Ni tampoco
al gobierno feliz de este monarca.
Ni a su cultura helénica, sus viajes
o la estabilidad de las fronteras
de su imperio. Percibo
aquello como patria,
como época propia,
porque intuyo que entonces no tendría
la sensación de exilio
creciente que despierta
en mí la época que me ha tocado,
la cultura angustiosa
dictada por algunos que no aman,
los intelectuales
de clase media, aquellos
que no son ni poetas ni filósofos,
el futuro nublado,
la situación incierta de mi patria.

The Reign of Hadrian

It's about, above all, a theory of knowledge,
of the manner in which a man steals himself little by
little from the ideas of his time which he rejects.
    Marguerite Yourcenar, [on Zeno], *Letter to Alain Bosquet,*
    January 1, 1964

The reign of Hadrian
is like the October the Japanese
celebrate. But the nostalgia
I feel from those years isn't a result
of the absence of gods. Nor is it due to
the joyful government of this monarch.
Nor to the Hellenic culture, his trips
or the stability of the borders
of his empire. I recognize
that as my homeland,
as my own time,
because I sense that then I wouldn't have
this feeling of deepening
exile that wakes
in me the age that I have been given,
the anguishing culture
dictated by some who don't love,
the intellectuals
of the middle class, those
who are neither poets nor philosophers,
the cloudy future,
the uncertain situation of my country.

Arte de Traducir

Debemos celebrar las traducciones afortunadas.
Como el *Précis de décomposition*
de Cioran, convertido
en *Breviario de podredumbre*.
En momentos de máxima inseguridad cultural
el arte de traducir se erige
en última forma de conocimiento.
Ahora que la torre de la historia
sufre asedios que pueden ser los definitivos,
hemos de recurrir a los especialistas
y a quienes los traducen
sin prisa y con audacia
intuyendo el sentido final de los escritos.
Para comprender todo
lo que ocurre estos años,
basta con este libro
de Arnaldo Momigliano
que trata de otra época:
The Alien Wisdom, que alguien bellamente
ha traducido *La sabiduría
de los bárbaros.*

The Art of Translation

We should celebrate the fortunate translations.
Like the *Précis de décomposition*
by Cioran, turned into
Breviary of Putrefaction.
In those moments of maximum cultural insecurity
the art of translation extends
into the ultimate form of knowledge.
Now that the tower of history
suffers sieges that can be definitive,
we should appeal to the specialists
and to those who translate them
slowly and boldly
intuiting the essential meaning of the writing.
In order to understand everything
that has happened these years,
it's enough to look at this book
by Arnaldo Momigliano
which is about another time:
The Alien Wisdom, which someone
translated beautifully into *La sabiduría
de los bárbaros.*

Jueves Santo

para Pablo García Baena

Aún estaban los cuerpos en la arena
de la orilla del agua dulcemente
fugitiva o un poco más acá
sobre la hierba, cuando se convierte
en ribera completamente urbana.
Aún estaban los cuerpos en la arena,
y pasaron los Cristos y Vírgenes
por el puente romano, verticales,
mientras abajo los horizontales
dilataban la siesta hasta las siete.
Caía el sol de abril tibio y benévolo.
Compartieron los pétalos, la música,
la marcha, las trompetas, los antiguos
timbales. El incienso no hacía
distinciones. Indicio de la gloria,
alcanzó a los desnudos como algo
natural, ni siquiera se movieron
en su principio de paganidad.
El caos católico. La apoteosis.
La yuxtaposición. El más perfecto
modo de conocer. De los contrarios
incluso incompatibles creen algunos
firmemente que son sólo sinónimos.
Aún estaban los cuerpos en la arena.

Holy Thursday

for Pablo García Baena

The bodies were still in the sand
at the edge of the water, sweetly
fugitive, or a little more over here
on the grass, when it turns into
a completely urban shore.
The bodies were still in the sand,
and the Christs and Virgins passed
over the Roman bridge, vertical,
while below the horizontal ones
stretched their nap until seven.
The April sun fell warm and benevolent.
They shared the petals, the music,
the march, trumpets, the old
kettledrums. The incense
didn't make distinctions. Signs of glory,
it reached the nudes like something
natural, they didn't even move
in their principled paganism.
Catholic chaos. The apotheosis.
The juxtaposition. The most perfect
way to know. Some believe, firmly
the contrary, even the incompatible,
are only synonyms.
The bodies were still in the sand.

Gimnasta

Utiliza expresiones como *tren superior,*
centímetros de brazo, horizontalidad.
Está arriesgando mucho sobre la barra fija.
No quiso practicar fútbol ni baloncesto.
Sus padres lo apuntaron de niño en un gimnasio.
Gira. Vuela. Organiza todos sus movimientos.
Sueña con pinchar música ante la muchedumbre
en una discoteca: Fabrik de Fuenlabrada,
la misma en la que baila cada noche de sábado.
La naturalidad es una de sus bazas.
En Pekín estará en su mejor momento.
Tendrá 23 años. Si no falla ahora mismo,
si convence a los jueces, dentro de unos instantes
va a gozar la alegría más sencilla del mundo.
Mañana tendrá acceso VIP en el aeropuerto.
Y será recibido por su alcalde, el de Móstoles.
Podrá pinchar su música ante su gente en Fabrik.
Ejercicio completo. Impecable salida.
Va a ser ya muy difícil que se le escape el oro.

Gymnast

He uses expressions like *upper body,*
arm centimeters, horizontality.
He's risking it on the high bar.
He didn't want to play football or basketball.
His parents signed him up with a gym as a child.
He spins. Flies. He plans each move.
He dreams of being a DJ in front of the crowd
in the dance club, Fabrik, in Fuenlabrada—
he dances there every Saturday night.
His natural movements are one of his strengths.
He'll be at the top of his game in Beijing.
He'll be 23. If he doesn't fail right now,
if he convinces the judges, in just a few moments
he'll enjoy the simplest pleasure in the world.
Tomorrow he'll have VIP access in the airport.
And the mayor will welcome him, the mayor of Móstoles.
He could DJ for his friends in Fabrik.
Exercise complete. Perfect dismount.
It will be hard for the gold to escape him.

In Joyful Memory

En alegre memoria. Que no haya
nada más que alegría en la memoria
de Duncan Charles Kirkpatrick, que pasó
sobre este mundo apenas veinte años.
Love is stronger than death. Así creemos.
Hemos cifrado nuestras esperanzas
en esa despojada certidumbre.
Así escribimos, sin saber muy bien
qué queremos decir, qué significan
esas raras palabras, repetidas
por las generaciones de los hombres.
Qué consecuencias tiene en lo concreto.
Pero es cierto. Es así. El amor es más.
Y triunfará de un modo misterioso.
Así ordenamos que se grabe en bronce:
el amore es más fuerte que la muerte.

En Alegre Memoria

In joyful memory. There should be
nothing more than happiness in the memory
of Duncan Charles Kirkpatrick, who passed
over this world hardly twenty years.
Love is stronger than death. That's what we believe.
We have coded our hopes
in this stripped down certainty.
That's how we write, without really knowing
what we want to say, what these
rare words mean, repeated
by the generations of men.
What consequences they have on the concrete.
But it's true. It's like this. Love is more.
And it will triumph in a mysterious way.
That's why we have it engraved in bronze:
love is stronger than death.

Hay Algo en el Amor

Hay algo en el amor que pertenece
a este mundo. En los múltiples
instantes en que todo
tiene sentido desde que llegaste,
en toda la materia de pronto convertida
en regalo, pradera que pisamos,
terraza que se asoma o muralla que guarda,
también en la dulzura de los días,
en la rutina humilde de tenerte
a mi lado,
lo noto.

Pero algo en el amor no es de este mundo.
Algo que no es abstracto.
Lo pruebo, por ejemplo, en la temperatura
de tu piel, cada vez que nos quedamos
dormidos juntos, y cada mañana
en que no espero más que tu primer
beso, cuando recobras
a ciegas tu lugar entre mis brazos.
Entonces se anticipa lo que un día tendremos
definitivamente.
Para poder nombrarlo
se me hace necesaria la noción de solsticio.
No lo razono más. Es una especie
de primicia.

There Is Something inside Love

There is something inside love that belongs
to this world. In the multiple
instances in which everything
makes sense since you arrived,
in all the material suddenly converted
to gift, the meadow we walk through,
the terrace overlooking or wall that protects,
also in the sweetness of days,
in the humble routine of having you
beside me,
I notice it.

But something inside love isn't of this world.
Something that isn't abstract.
I try it, for example, in the warmth
of your skin, every time we fall asleep
together, and every morning
that I hope for nothing more than your first
kiss, when you recover
your place in my arms blindly.
Then we anticipate what one day we will have
definitively.
In order to name it,
the notion of solstice seems necessary to me.
I won't reason this over any more. It is a kind
of first fruit.

Notes

[from the Introduction]

The poet, in discussion with the translator, attempted to clarify these notions by adding the following: "I used to consider myself a Catholic by culture...but someone who lives fully in the world of culture cannot use culturally as if it were a restriction, but as a plenitude. I accept that I am Catholic, because I am. The same way I am a Roman, a Greek, a modern educated man. Roman and Catholic are almost synonymous in some languages, like in English. And I'm something like that, but in a different way. I am pagan and Christian. As a pagan I behave with naturalness. As a Christian, I am careful that this naturalness is respectful of others. As a pagan I think that everything should be expressed. As a Christian, I try not to say things that might harm others, though I am faithful to my obligations as a poet. I am a pagan and Christian like Michelangelo, for example. Or Botticelli. I think about Michelangelo's *David* and *Pietà*. I think many stories about art say that Michelangelo was Catholic and gay."

Time Begets Decades

Titus Livy was a historian who composed the extensive history of Rome called *Ab Urbe Condita Libri*, which documented Rome from its founding (approximately 753 BC). In this poem the poet uses "decades" to allude to both Livy's ten book history of Rome and how Livy's books discussed the lives of famous Romans in ten year increments, in the way that Niccolo Machiavelli, for example, wrote his *Discourses on the First Decade of Titus Livius*.

The Eyes of the Ascetic

The last line is drawn from a poem about Felipe II by Álvaro Mutis, the Columbian poet, novelist, and essayist.

Difficultly

Lorenzo the Magnificent, also known as Lorenzo de' Medici, was a diplomat, politician and patron of scholars, artists, and poets. He lived at the height of the early Italian Renaissance, and his death marked the end of the Golden Age of Florence. He helped maintain peace between various Italian states, but this collapsed upon his death. Lorenzo was also an excellent poet, as was typical of a man of his status during the Renaissance.

Vltimus Romanorum

The description "Last of the Romans" (*Vltimus Romanorum*) has historically been given to any man thought to embody the values of Ancient Roman civilization—values which, by implication, became extinct on his death.

Correspondence

Marcus Aurelius, Roman Emperor from 161 to his death in 180, was the last of the "Five Good Emperors." Marcus Cornelius Fronto (c. 100-170) was a Roman grammarian and rhetorician. In this poem, Fronto calls Marcus Aurelius "Domino," or "My Lord," and Marcus Aurelius calls Fronto "Magistro," or "Master," which means "that he is more" (magis). Like *Eros is more*, "Magistro" is more than "Domino," "Master is more than Lord."

The Reign of Hadrian

Hadrian was a Roman governor during the second century AD, and he inspired, along with Marcus Aurelius, *The Memoirs of Hadrian* by Marguerite Yourcenar, a book quite present in the writing of *Eros Is More*.

The Art of Translation

The book, *A Short History of Decay*, was written by Emil Cioran (April 8, 1911 – June 20, 1995), a Romanian philosopher and essayist, and translated into Spanish by the celebrated philosopher Fernando Savater. Arnaldo Momigliano, is an Italian historian known for his work in historiography. The Spanish version of Momigliano's book is loosely translated as *The Wisdom of the Barbarians*.

RECENT TITLES FROM ALICE JAMES BOOKS

Mad Honey Symposium, Sally Wen Mao
Split, Cathy Linh Che
Money Money Money | Water Water Water, Jane Mead
Orphan, Jan Heller Levi
Hum, Jamaal May
Viral, Suzanne Parker
We Come Elemental, Tamiko Beyer
Obscenely Yours, Angelo Nikolopoulos
Mezzanines, Matthew Olzmann
Lit from Inside: 40 Years of Poetry from Alice James Books, Edited by
    Anne Marie Macari and Carey Salerno
Black Crow Dress, Roxane Beth Johnson
Dark Elderberry Branch: Poems of Marina Tsvetaeva, A Reading by
    Ilya Kaminsky and Jean Valentine
Tantivy, Donald Revell
Murder Ballad, Jane Springer
Sudden Dog, Matthew Pennock
Western Practice, Stephen Motika
me and Nina, Monica A. Hand
Hagar Before the Occupation | Hagar After the Occupation, Amal al-
    Jubouri
Pier, Janine Oshiro
Heart First into the Forest, Stacy Gnall
This Strange Land, Shara McCallum
lie down too, Lesle Lewis
Panic, Laura McCullough
Milk Dress, Nicole Cooley
Parable of Hide and Seek, Chad Sweeney
Shahid Reads His Own Palm, Reginald Dwayne Betts
How to Catch a Falling Knife, Daniel Johnson
Phantom Noise, Brian Turner
Father Dirt, Mihaela Moscaliuc

ALICE JAMES BOOKS has been publishing poetry since 1973. The press was founded in Boston, Massachusetts as a cooperative wherein authors performed the day-to-day undertakings of the press. This collaborative element remains viable even today, as authors who publish with the press are also invited to become members of the editorial board and participate in editorial decisions at the press. The editorial board selects manuscripts for publication via the press's annual, national competition, the Alice James Award. Alice James Books seeks to support women writers and was named for Alice James, sister to William and Henry, whose extraordinary gift for writing went unrecognized during her lifetime.

DESIGNED BY MIKE BURTON

PRINTED BY BookMobile

··